Basia and Dominik,
enjoy the
Whispering of Angels
and most of all ...
enjoy baby.

With love,
Marie.

Whispering of Angels

Affirmations for the Child in Your Life

Annalee Ash

HAMPTON ROADS
PUBLISHING COMPANY, INC.

for the evolving human spirit

Dedication

This little book is dedicated to you.
May you feel the joy, love, and comfort
of your Heavenly Father and Mother.
Please, share it with others.
You will change the world.

Introduction

Only one day left and it was time to leave my shelter of twenty-eight days. Twenty-eight days in rehab, and I was there to discover why I had gained forty pounds as a result of overeating after I had stopped drinking two years before. Others were there for alcohol or drug recovery, or depression. The substance did not matter; we all had similar core beliefs about ourselves that led to the numbing of our emotions in one form or another.

"We learn our survival skills by the age of six," the director told us. This comment started my mind rolling. How was this possible? Survival skills learned by age six. Incredible!

Then the group exercise. So simple. So powerful. A total expression of love. The result? This book. I participated, observing what was occurring around me. The group involved both men and women, ages eighteen to late sixties. Age and gender did not matter when it came to receiving these simple messages. *"Oh, the whole world deserves to have this experience, to hear these words,"* I thought. The messages were so simple, who would ever think they could affect us so deeply.

As I felt male bravado crumble beneath the touch of my hands on the shoulders of one man when I whispered to him, "God smiled the day you were born," I knew somehow I would bring these messages to others. The still small voice was louder and clearer than ever before: "*Everyone needs to hear this over and over and over.*" As I continued around the circle of these lovely souls, I watched their faces as expressions softened and eyes closed. Tears gently rolled down cheeks as they heard and felt deep within the messages they had not heard in years. Perhaps they had never heard them at all and yearned to; perhaps they realized they had not spoken these words to their loved ones in years. It did not matter. Loving, caring spirit filled the room and the heart of every person present. I would never be the same.

Miracles happen in times like this. I knew this was the reason I was inspired to stay two more days. It was my birthday. What a gift. A gift for the world. I did not sleep that night. I sat up and put the experience on paper.

I checked the coursework from the workshop. The inspiring messages were typed on a piece of paper, no name or publications credited. I had read many of these words in various books, but I decided to edit the experience, combine it with other messages I heard during the thirty days, and put it in book form.

It had felt like angels were speaking these words to us, and it felt so personal that I decided I would hand write my book . . . in gold ink . . . celestial and beautiful. *Golden Moments on Angels' Wings* . . . the original name just flowed onto the paper.

My sister received the first copy for Christmas. Friends soon started requesting copies after receiving them as gifts, and then insisting that I publish my little book. Nevertheless, there is more to the story.

I recall thinking: "*These are the words that babies should hear from the time they are in the womb, after they are born, through childhood and adolescence into adulthood.*" What an incredible shift could take place if we all heard these messages before age six and then carried them with us.

Imagine the incredible effect if you heard, "I love you just the way you are" as a child, as a teenager, as an adult. I currently have a handful of women friends from ages twenty-six to the late sixties who are still affected by early memories of verbal and nonverbal messages that they were ugly little girls, or that they weren't loved the way they should have been loved. Imagine for a moment, you as a baby, a teenager, hearing someone whisper to you, "I am so happy you are here" or, "I've waited so long for you." Imagine yourself as a baby hearing someone lovingly whisper to you, "I want to nurture you, to bathe you, to wrap you in a warm blanket and hold you." Imagine yourself as a teenager hearing, "It is okay for you to be different and to have your own views" or, "I will be here for you to test your boundaries, and discover your limits" and, "I love you just the way you are." Just imagine.

We must reach out to others, children and adults alike, and express the love toward each other that we long for in ourselves.

Mother Theresa and Princess Diana were our contemporary teachers. They showed us how simple it is. A touch. A smile. Kind words. These women are gone, yet their example remains. Now we must carry on.

The message is so simple. We have heard it time and time again. "Love one another, as I have loved you." The message was given almost 2000 years ago, and slowly we are awakening to listen and obey.

I believe we are born in a state of grace filled with divine love.

I have experienced this on more than one occasion, taking newborn babies in my arms and whispering these messages to them. Newborn babies, who supposedly cannot focus, cannot see, suddenly become very alert and focused on me when I hold them and begin speaking softly to them these loving words that I know they will carry within themselves.

It takes love, most simply. Every culture can experience this; every country, all people. To love, not judge. To love, not criticize. To love, no matter what our vocation is, no matter what path we follow in life, no matter how difficult—we are to love one another.

This little book in its simplicity can be read at many levels. For some, it may be from parent to child, grandparent to child, friend to friend, or from the Creator to the child in us all. Some may feel it is God speaking. It certainly is possible. I feel the words are inspired. They have taken many forms before, from books to bumper stickers. The rehab has been closed, but the experience remains.

I lovingly pray that each one of you will share these words with those you know, those you meet, with those you love and with those you wish to love. God Bless.

In love and grace.

Annalee

Acknowledgments

"God does not inspire unattainable inspirations."
—St. Thérèse of Lisieux

"I will go and do the things the Lord hath commanded, for I know the Lord giveth no commandments . . . save he shall prepare a way for them that they may accomplish the thing which he commanded them."
—1 Nephi 3:6, Book of Mormon

I want to acknowledge events and persons that have led me to present this book to the public. Events that to some may seem coincidental. However, I do not believe in accidents or coincidences. I know that these moments were guided and inspired, and miraculously I was aware enough to recognize what was occurring, and to listen to the angels whispering to me.

The notion of angels (spirit guides) is known throughout many religions and spiritual paths, and yet it is often questioned and even scorned. Recently, it suddenly dawned on me that during some of my darkest moments, my solace came to me in the form of roses. Sometimes upon feeling a sense of comfort and peace, I became aware that there was a statue or shrine to St. Thérèse nearby. I have been most aware of St. Thérèse since I was about fifteen years old and I realize that her presence and guidance in my life has been most apparent in the last sixteen years.

> ". . . and I will do my greatest works on Earth, from Heaven, from whence I shall shower the Earth with roses."
>
> —St. Thérèse (age 24)

It seems to me that when I am living in the present moment and not obsessed with worrying about my future or lamenting about my past, I am able to discern the opportunities presented to me. I am also keenly aware of noticing the significance of past events and how I was guided and protected in various circumstances.

There have been three significant occurrences, related to this book, during which I know she, St. Thérèse, has been with me to encourage and to inspire me. The first instance was in rehab. After hearing of my encounters with St. Thérèse, the director called me into her office, whereupon she showed me her "shrine," a lovely statue of St. Thérèse and a fresh bouquet of roses. It was there in rehab that I was first inspired to write this little book.

When pondering the publication of this book, it always seemed too simple to be significant enough to publish, although I believed the message shared is supposed to be simple. Again, the thought came to me how humbling true love is. The simplicity of the message unites us all; no one need feel left out. St. Thérèse, in her desire to teach us all to love our Creator taught us as a child. We have all experienced those precious moments spent with children when absolute pearls—gems of wisdom—are spoken from their tiny, earnest, and honest hearts, and we look at them sometimes in wonderment as to how they can utter such wisdom. In following St. Thérèse's example, I found the courage to bring this humble little book to the world. I needed a publisher.

Hence, the next significant moment came when I was in Chicago, while attending a publisher's and book seller's convention; a publisher actually asked to see my book. I hesitated momentarily, faced the fear of rejection, took a deep breath, and handed over my copy. My collection of three books is called *Golden Graces*, and my original acknowledgment was simply to St. Thérèse. Morgan DeLeo was my angel that day; she, too, seemed stunned upon reading my acknowledgement. Her publishing company is Grace Publishing and Communications, and she, also, showed me her "shrine," a bouquet of roses sitting behind her display, to her angel, St. Thérèse. Morgan was my first professional confirmation that this book must be published.

Four years had passed since I had initially written my first copy, and as the days rolled into weeks, months, and years, it became apparent to me that all my fears and doubts regarding this book applied to my life. I trusted I would be guided through diligent prayer as to when the time would be appropriate to seek publication. I was looking for the right time, in the worldly sense, when people would readily accept the message I felt so inspired to share. Frustration set in as I continued to pursue my career in the hospitality industry without the hope of ever having time to pursue my real dreams.

Late one night, while walking with a friend through the streets of Georgetown, I decided to take drastic measures. The next day I turned in my request for a personal leave of absence. It intuitively seemed the right thing to do. When asked by my manager if my health was okay, if there was any way he could help me, I told him about my little book. I told him I simply felt strongly that now was the time to focus on my book and find a publisher. Period. He heard me loud and clear.

Later that evening, my decision was confirmed. As I attended evening meditation and service at the chapel at Georgetown University, the priest began the service acknowledging the joyful celebration of the feast day of St. Thérèse of Lisieux. My two colleagues and I were stunned. They knew of my relationship with St. Thérèse, had even given me books on her life and teachings. All three of us knew our lives would be changed. This confirmed without out a doubt that I had made the right decision. I felt a surge of strength and courage and the presence of peace in my heart.

St. Thérèse, the first modern-day saint, entered the Carmelite convent at age fifteen and died from tuberculosis at age twenty-four. Her sole mission was to become as a child of God, to love God, and make Him known and loved. In the year she died, she finally understood the meaning of the second commandment, "You shall love your neighbor as yourself . . . and that as I have loved you, you are to love one another."

Herein lies the premise for my little book. These gentle words, written on the following pages, spoken with love, will fill your souls to overflowing. I can promise you that anyone who hears these words from you will feel loved beyond measure, and you too will feel a love you cannot begin to imagine when you read them to yourself or take the risk to share them. We can begin to change the world, for if we can begin again to love one another as children love—with trust and without judgment—we too can feel the inexplicable joy that our heavenly Father desires for us.

My love to St. Thérèse for confirming this love in my heart.

I am filled with gratitude to Louise Hay, Melanie Beattie, Marianne Williamson, Janet Greeson, Carol Black, Hazelden, the authors of *The Blue Book*, *The Little Red Book*, *Twenty-Four Hours a Day*, and Wayne Dyer, Neale Donald Walsch, Deepak Chopra, Bernie Segal, Harry Palmer, Phyllis Ozarin, and others—all whose inspiring messages helped me to understand this earthly existence. My queen-sized bed used to be covered with their books, as I searched for answers. These books have lovingly been passed on to friends traveling the same journey.

Perhaps it is no coincidence that this book is being published at the end of this century. We are beginning the new millennium with the ability to make a difference in a most simple way.

Whispering of Angels

God smiled
the day you were born.

Welcome

to the world.

Thank you for joining us.

I have been waiting
so long for you.

In all the world
there has never been
another like you.

I am so happy you are here . . .

. . . and I am so happy you are you.

I've prepared
a special place
for you to live.

Your needs are
okay with me.

I want to nurture you;
to bathe you,
to wrap you in a warm
blanket and hold you,
to clothe you
and feed you.

You are perfect
in every way.

I'll give you
all the time you need
to have your needs met.

I will not leave you.

You make such

a difference in my life.

It is okay
to be curious,
to want to look,
to touch,
to taste.

I'll make it safe
for you to explore.

I am here
to take care
of your needs.
You don't have to
take care of mine.

It is okay for you to be taken care of.

It is okay
to say no.

It is okay
for both of us
to be mad.
We will work
our problems out.

I am glad you want
to be you.

It is okay
to feel scared
when you do things
your way.

It is okay to feel sad
when things don't
work out for you.

You can still be you
and count on my
being there for you.

I love
watching you learn
to grow up,
to talk, to walk.

It is okay
for you to
think for yourself.

It is okay
for you to be different,
to have
your own views.

You can think
about your feelings . . .

. . . and have feelings
about what
you are thinking.

I will be here for you
to test your boundaries
and to discover
your limits.

I'll set limits for you
to help you find out
who you are.

You can ask for what
you want
one hundred percent
of the time.

It is okay to cry.

You are not responsible
for other
people's actions.

You can ask
questions
if something
confuses you.

You can stand up
for yourself
and
I'll support you.

You can trust your inner wisdom, your feelings.

You can talk
about your feelings.

It is okay to be afraid.
We can talk
about your fears.

Only God
can be your judge.

Other's judgment
and criticism of you
is none of your business.
Do not let it upset you.

You
are a precious child
of God.

You are worthy
of receiving all that
the Heavenly Father
has planned for you . . .

. . . and He does have a very special plan for you.

Be happy,
joyous,
and free
to be you!

Be creative!

Take risks!

You can do things
your own way!

You can trust
your judgment.

Expect miracles.

You are a miracle.

I love you
just the way
you are.

Biography

"Life has never been boring," says Annalee Ash. "From the day I was born it has been an adventure." Her terrified parents dodged the Autobahn Bandits on the main auto route in Germany from Bavaria to the hospital in Munich. Since then Annalee has moved forty times—all in the northeast United States. "I've been privileged to travel in the U.S., Saudi Arabia, Bahrain, South America, and Europe. It has been those experiences, along with living in New England, Manhattan, and the eastern end of Long Island that have opened my eyes and my heart to accepting the differences and celebrating the similarities in the world. It is fascinating to experience other cultures and traditions. Life is really so incredibly enriching wherever we go."

A graduate of the University of Vermont, Annalee has spent her life on a spiritual journey, all the while learning to listen to the angels. "So often we ignore the messages, the promptings; but when we are conscious, living in the moment, it is amazing to see and experience the glorious opportunities presented to us."

Hampton Roads Publishing Company

. . . for the evolving human spirit

Hampton Roads Publishing Company
publishes books on a variety of subjects including
metaphysics, health, complementary medicine,
visionary fiction, and other related topics.

For a copy of our latest catalog,
call toll-free, 800-766-8009,
or send your name and address to:

Hampton Roads Publishing Company, Inc.
134 Burgess Lane
Charlottesville, VA 22902
e-mail: hrpc@hrpub.com
www.hrpub.com